Words of Truth

Nathan Morgan

Ozark Publishing, LLC

Contents

Prologue

Through this book, my goal is to shed enlightenment to the reader. I pray my testimony can help those that's lost find their way and hopefully lead others to Christ. Personally, I've tried to see opportunities, or a chance for growth, through all of my life experiences, and I'll like my wisdom I've found to help others think more positively. I believe that with the right amount of willpower and faith, miracles occur.

I hope through all my endeavors and all my writings that I end up making the world a better place. I'm grateful for this opportunity to be heard. I want to thank God for providing me with this knowledge. I believe that treating others with compassion goes a long way. I believe as Christians we should try to be as Christ like as possible and remember, God is love.

My birthday is June 24th ,1993, I started writing music when I was 17. My artist name is Phoenix 11. My hometown is Van Buren, Missouri, but as a kid I moved a lot. This gave me the chance to see different environments and culture and weigh pros and cons about the city and country life.

I'm the youngest of 3 siblings: I have an older brother and sister. I try to stay positive no matter what, because I believe perspective is key. I really enjoy writing; I see beauty in expressing my thoughts. I'm all about playing my part, you could say I'm purpose driven, and I believe that getting this book out is part of my purpose, so I'm content.

I got in a car accident on June 19, 2004, was in a coma for 5 days and awakened the morning of June 24, 2004 (my 11th birthday.) It took me about 3 years to bounce back mentally from my Traumatic Brain Injury but what the devil planned to be a curse God turned into a blessing because it left me with a powerful testimony. Long story short, I went to a church camp right before this car accident and the pastor told everyone that he had a vision 5 nights in a row that someone will get into a car accident when they left and have a near death or death experience and he wanted to lead them to Christ before this happened. Well, I prayed and asked God if He existed to prove Himself because I needed to know if He existed.

Chapter One

Greatness, Grace and God's Love

G reatness is formed through tribulation. Love is acquired through God's presence and grace. Understanding develops trust. True friendship is more valuable than gold, for it is priceless. A Wiseman understands his own, as with a fool: to a fool a Wiseman is silly, and vice versa.

To an extent a person can only be as smart as God allows them to be, but their faith and intent are X factors in that equation. One should find balance in almost everything. Saving a lost soul is more powerful than taking vengeance out on an enemy, for your previous worst enemy could become your future best friend. You have more of an effect on others than you even know, your voice will change the world to a degree, your faith and how much you include God into your plan will determine what degree that is. One should be careful what they focus on, for what one mentally digests alters/becomes their thoughts; and one's thoughts are the backbone of one's reality, for they transition to your words and actions, and that's essential, for one's words and actions define oneself. An idea is more powerful than you think, for it can change the world. It's better to be a poor kid with knowledge than an old, wicked king. Righteousness is maintained by keeping good principles.

God's love, (the Holy Spirit) is that void inside that everyone's looking to fill, lust provides an illusion for it temporally fills the void, but in the end just makes it worse. God's love is unconditional, but we can still make God angry: one should be fearful of doing things in spite. A pure heart is more valuable than a crown of gold. Wicked thoughts are one's device of destruction, but loving thoughts make up the structure of a Wiseman's

Empire. God gave everyone a spiritual gift, but what good is a gift if you don't take the time and effort to metaphorically open it up? Loving words are soothing to a listener's soul, but hateful words cause division and come from an unstable person.

If you don't pick a path, then a path will be chosen for you. If one has a role model it should be Jesus, or one that is Christ like. Only God knows the depths of one's heart; that's reason enough not to judge another. Don't let your doubt blind you but allow your faith to set you free. Genuine love is the everlasting victory. Compassion is greater than hate, but in a world such as this, it's a rarer characteristic.

One shouldn't go to a strip club looking to find true love, just like one shouldn't pray to the devil to find love and peace: if you're seeking something look in the appropriate place.

The biggest battles are fought in the mind. Hardships create testimonies, testimonies can save other's lives, but how we respond to our hardships determines if we become more fruitful or bitter.

We are refined through our tribulations, like a sword that a Blacksmith forges in fire. Let me emphasize on the fact that how we perceive these hardships will determine if we become something strong, something our creator can use, or if we break under the pressure and heat of our trial like some swords do. Love lasts and endures, while lust fades away and leaves one longing.

How you build a house determines the quality of the home: for instance, if you build a friendship with (spiritually) good fruit then you get a good lasting relationship, but if you build it with bad fruit then you get a destructive and toxic relationship. It is better to pray for wisdom than it is to act on the vain desires of one's heart.

Put your hope in Christ and you'll receive the desires of your heart, but it never says you'll receive it right away, patience is key. Is a mistake really a mistake if you learn from it? Or could one classify it as a hard lesson? But one shouldn't repeat failure. Most of the time the harder path leads to a greater road.

A system has multiple functions, and it is written, 'in God's eye's we're equal' here, let me elaborate, let's say a person's purpose in life is to donate five dollars to a charity, while another's purpose is to preach the word of God to billions and ends up spiritually saving millions of lives. Now a person would think that the one who preached to billions was more important than the one who donated the five dollars. But what if I told you that at one point in time the one that was to preach to billions was starving to death and would have died if the other wouldn't have donated the five dollars to that charity? God made us all and gave us all a unique purpose, I'm here to tell you that our purpose might be different, but it is equal.

The direction of one's drive determines where they end up: the path to heaven is straight and narrow, meaning it's harder to get to, but won't the reward be worth all the effort? It's better to be simple and kind, then complex and mischievous. One that endures more tribulation receives a greater reward. One that saves a soul adds to his spiritual cup. Insight shared with friends outweighs knowledge withheld from foes. Trust is hard to gain, but easy to lose.

One can do good things with money, but the reason people say it's the root of all evil is because earthly riches produce obsession, obsession creates greed, while greed is the real root of all evil.

From the words of Bob Marley: "People say they love the wind, but when it blows, they close the window. People say they love the Sun, but when it shines, they hide under a shade tree. People say they love the rain, but when it comes down, they cover themselves with an umbrella; that's why when people say they love me, I get afraid."

A man with great faith, and strong will, will out do a stubborn genius. It is better to suffer for a cause, than it is to become bountiful from corruption. This life will pass away, but no one can put a measure on eternity, what's salvation worth to you?

Could you find it in yourself to go through unspeakable pain for a world that rejected you? Because that's what Jesus did for us all. It's better to be criticized for Christ's sake, then to be praised for the wrong reasons. It is better to have little and be content, than to have abundance and be greedy.

The effect I can have is worth the trials I have to endure. Experience is the best teacher. It shows true strength to keep a kind heart in a cruel world. Strong determination is the structure of a legacy. A hero is defined by a moment. Be careful of the words you use, because you can build someone up, or tear them down through them.

It is better for this world to forget you, than to remember you for something terrible. One that truly has God in their heart, overall, will be loving and kind. One should make the most out of every situation, but reaping well out of a bad situation is like receiving a crown of honor. Only a fool looks for trouble, a Wiseman looks for peace, but if finds trouble looks for solutions. A Wiseman thinks ahead and proceeds with caution, while a fool jumps right into scenarios, then gets confused by the chain of events. Read, pray, do the works of God, etc. one should find a good balance: be smart when managing your time. Sequence is essential.

Insight captivates, knowledge is power, and wisdom, few gain over time. Abundance of faith is more powerful than abundance of physical strength.

Shame is what one receives when they waste a spiritual gift. Everyone wants to find love, but previous disappointments can blur the vision of one's real desire. Your pride will tell you that you want people to look up to you, but your soul says, you just want to be accepted. One that finds equality soulful and pleasing is good. The aspects you seek to find in a person will be the characteristics that stand out. Know when to act, and know when to meditate, just like a flower: you don't want to water it too much or too little. Creativity makes one unique. Perspective is key, blessed is the man who creates a testimony out of a hardship. The greater the purpose God has for one, the harder the struggle they must endure. Talent is a blessing, but when wasted, it feels like a curse.

God's plan might be mysterious, but it is what's best for us. God knows us better than we know ourselves. Most people are products of their environment; few make their environment a product of them. Most people are so greatly influenced by their environment that it defines who they are; but some are so mentally stable that they change their environment, For instance, Jesus hung around sinners but changed them instead of allowing them to change him.

In the bible it says, 'God see's end to beginning, beginning to end', meaning He knows what's going to happen before it happens. My question is why did he make the devil? My answer can be sectioned in three different reasons: He gave everyone freewill; the devil used his freewill to turn against God. One can't fully appreciate the good without them knowing the other side: the principle of someone with a silver spoon in their mouth, they have always been given everything, you could buy them a new Lamborghini but they might not care, they might have ten more, but you buy a homeless man a new pair of shoes and he'll be eternally grateful. And life's ultimately a test; we're given a lot of choices and challenges to see if we're worthy of heaven. God don't make mistakes.

A lot of people think that the New Testament and the Old Testament contradict each other because in the Old you have a wrathful God, and in the new you got a loving God. But let me explain how although that's true, they still don't contradict each other. I believe God made everyone pure and good, but over time we're all guilty of metaphorically losing our way and leaning into sinful desires, turning against God and/or blaming Him, basically giving into the ways of the world. I believe that overtime people have made God angry, remember it says, 'God is slow to anger,' but we can still make Him angry. In the Old Testament you seen God's response to us offending Him. But Jesus came, overcame the world and temptation, and then died for what we all deserve. This made a new covenant and showed God that there's hope for mankind: The result of Jesus' amazing legacy is God's unconditional love.

Chapter Two

Being a Real Man

Having a curious heart isn't a bad thing, but one should know what matters to question and when to question them. Faith, hope, and love is the structure of righteousness. More wisdom results in more opportunities. A real man can create peace from the chaos. Life can get hard no matter what, "long suffering is a fruit of the spirit," and "God makes it rain on the wicked and just alike." God never promised that it would be easy: sometimes the best rewards in life are the hardest to achieve.

Truth be told the Devil's a powerful entity, but God is more powerful than anything else. Also, God is more powerful than everything else put together.

When an idea is just an idea, the value of it is in the eye of the beholder: but once it takes form, then its true value is revealed. Humbleness is built through patience. Intent listening grows understanding. The structure of righteousness is hard to form, but if/when achieved it is pleasing to have.

Love is the most powerful emotion. What's amazing is the bible says, 'God is love.' Now God can choose to be anything He wants to be not only does He choose to be the most powerful thing, but it's also the best thing the He chooses to be, love. It takes time for a flower to bloom, just like it takes time for love to grow. Amazement is the result of beating the odds. To become elite, you have got to full heartedly practice the thing you're trying to master.

I believe the laws of physics correlate greatly to how people function: the law of physics state, 'an object at rest will stay at rest, an object in motion will stay in motion, meaning if a person decides to sit around idly for an extensive period of time then they become lazy, but a person that becomes active for an extensive amount of time more than likely they'll stay active. We're creatures of habit.

Finding true love is like finding a needle in a haystack, it might take a lot of time and effort to find, so if/when you find it try not to lose it. You can't satisfy everyone else, and you have got to live with the choices you make. Find out what matters most to you. Acts of peace are pleasing to the soul.

If you spell live backwards you get evil, I don't believe that's just a coincidence. I believe one becomes evil if/when they metaphorically lose their way of living. If society shuns or disappoints you, then this could affect how you think and act: you could end up doing something very bad, and maybe subconsciously a reason why you did it was to get back into society. I mean after someone gets convicted of a server crime they end up in prison or a mental hospital; they find themselves around a lot of other people.

The grass isn't greener on the other side of the fence, its greener where you water it: meaning relationships require work from both ends, and when you have a dispute try to meet in the middle. The hardest ones to love are the ones that need it the most. It's better to be a walking example than it is to force your religion on someone else.

You can lie to your friends, you can lie to your parents, you can even lie to yourself, but you can't lie to God. Scripture states, 'God don't call the equipped, He equips the called,' so when we see a mess of a person, God could see a masterpiece in the works. Every fire gets started by a spark. Boredom is a recipe for trouble.

Distractions can be good or bad, depending on what you're being distracted from and what the distraction is.

In the bible it states that, 'we are all parts of the body of Christ,' how I best understand that is: let's say you buy a car, mankind might tell you that the motor is worth $1,000, the gas tank is worth $75, and an electric cord is worth a few dollars, but don't you need all those essential parts for it to function/fulfill its purpose? Now if you thought about what I'm saying here, couldn't one say that the parts are of equal value since you need each one to fulfill its own unique purpose? That's the difference in how people see one's purpose, and how God see's it: people metaphorically put those 'price tags' on everyone's purpose, while God knows that everyone's purpose is required in order to complete a bigger picture.

There's a time when Michael Jordan first picked up a basketball, there was a time when Tiger Woods first stepped onto a golf course, even the greats had to start at some point in time: to excel in something it takes time and hard work. You will never know how good you'll be at something until you start doing it: take the first step.

Finding true love is worth all previous disappointing relationships. A bitter soul pushes away what they need the most: love. We accept what we think we deserve. One must love themselves in order to love another, but it is bad to love yourself too much: one shouldn't become obsessed with themselves: balance is key.

One that has a good spirit and open mind can learn a lot. The Holy Spirit brings much joy. One that becomes Christ-like eliminates hate in their loved one's hearts. Power can be earned, given, or taken away. One shouldn't become jealous of someone they like or love because it causes division.

Instead of being jealous just become motivated to do better. A metaphorical far reach is the combination of good hope and talent. When one receives just a taste of God's brilliance everyone is amazed. Love is the cure: when I say love I mean good will, righteousness, kindness, and purity. One that is truly Christ-like would be an epitome of a good person. A lot of the time you'll never see the effect you have on others; it's like planting a seed, and you don't see the first steps of its growth. Sometimes what you do or say might not have any effect on someone else at that point in time but could have a major effect on them later.

I have seen beautiful people become ugly, and ugly people become beautiful. Would you rather be with someone that has a beautiful personality, but just alright looks, or someone that has a beautiful appearance, but an ugly personality?

Hypothetically there were two construction workers, one hated their job and always complained about it because they saw it as hard work and very monotonous, while the other person loved it, they seen that they were building houses for other people, knowing people needed to live somewhere and took pride in their work, they claimed that they could come by the house 30 years in the future and (if a storm didn't wipe it out) could see it still standing tall: perspective is key.

An old adventurous person will have many stories to tell. Imagine how boring it would be if everyone was the same? The beauty of it is everyone is unique; your metaphorical true colors could shine brighter than you think. No one could completely understand the depths of God's brilliance, for instance there's around 7.5 billion people in the world and everyone's unique to a degree: no two are exactly alike, not even twins.

Chapter Three

Hope is Essential

Self-control is a strong element of power: the most lethal person you know could also be the kindest. Everyone feels emotions, don't look down on yourself when you feel bad ones; your response determines everything. Happiness is a product of true love. Righteousness is the product of the mixture of goodwill, humbleness, and long suffering. Hard work and a clear mind normally result in prosperity. One moment can change your life.

If you know you have a lot of potential at something, don't let anyone else discourage you from putting in the time and effort it takes to morph that potential into talent: but (in this context) be realistic with yourself. Boredom can be a result of too much wasted time. Would you rather live for nothing, or die for something? An innocent mind is peaceful.

Hope is essential, I believe that the loss of hope is the reason for most, if not all, suicides. The power of change lies within oneself. We are here to love one another, establish a relationship with God, and make memories. You and God might be the only ones that know what your intent is, but remember that everything is ultimately between you and God: so make sure your intent is pure.

Miracles are the result of God's goodness and one's immense faith. Everyone sees others in metaphorical different lights: who you think is a good person, I might think otherwise of, but the more Christ-like one becomes, the more people will notice their goodness. Love attracts, hate repels. God doesn't intend for anyone to go to hell, but does believe in what's right is right, and what's wrong is wrong, so in the end we'll either be rewarded or punished for how we ultimately lived our lives. But God's ways are mysterious to man: we have no idea exactly how anyone else is doing on this metaphorical test called life, that's another reason not to judge anyone else. But remember the thief on the cross, Jesus' grace alone can be enough to make it to heaven; although this is true one should be fearful in taking advantage of God.

One should use religion as a compass instead of interoperating everything the bible says literally, let the principles spoken in it morph your soul. If every Christian was Christ-like, then the world would be such a better place. I don't know why anyone would waste all kinds of time and effort pretending to be something they're not, if someone is unhappy with who they are, to me it makes more sense that they'll put that time and effort into changing.

Everyone wants to fulfill their purpose, most never know what it is, some fulfill it without even knowing they fulfilled it. Take away someone's meaning and you take away their reason to live.

We ultimately do what we think will bring us joy, but we can be wrong at times. One question, since God made us, then wouldn't He be the source of true joy? One could strive for more and be content with what they have at the same time: meaning if what I have now is all I will ever have, then I'll still be happy, but I'm also curious to find out what more I can achieve.

Accepting God into your heart opens the door to love. A person that is very insightful, has a good spirit, and is gifted attracts an interested crowd. All pastors should aim to have a big effect over necessarily having a big church.

An artist's music is an expression of their soul. A chaotic life makes one more likely to become unstable, but finding or creating the right solutions in bad situations increases one's cognitive ability. It sounds so easy to just be yourself, but some people never find out who they really are because truth be told it can be a hard task. It takes a lot of time, effort, and soul searching to find one's true self. One should prefer to have a big effect on others instead of necessarily having a big bank account. Good priorities is the root of stability. Positive priorities are the root of righteousness. Hope heals. A strong vision fuels determination. One voice can change the world. The devil will try to give the most doubt to the ones with the biggest purpose, the chosen ones need to listen to the voice of truth and lean into logic and reasoning. One who initially finds meaning finds joy, but the fear of losing meaning creates stress.

A positive soul, in combination with a bright mind, creates radiant thoughts. Everyone has a little good in them, showing others loving-kindness nurtures their good side, thus forth this can transition into them presenting a better version of themselves. God's in control, it's good to strive to be productive, but one shouldn't feel overwhelmed with obligations, find balance. No one besides Jesus is perfect. But remember that Jesus still felt emotions, there's a time when he flipped the tables over in the synagogue than told the people that they made His Father's house a den of thieves, I'm pretty sure He was very angry. Those people needed to change, although Jesus felt all human emotions, I believe that He always responded in the right manner. Once in scripture someone called Jesus a good man, but He stopped him and replied that no man is good, the only one that's good is His Father who is in heaven: I believe He said that because He was amazingly humble, and He knew that this test called life wasn't over for Him yet; although He never sinned or messed up, He still was capable of it. He didn't want to get ahead of Himself, because when someone gets ahead of themselves, they increase their likelihood of failure. To a huge degree your reality is based off how you perceive things: focus on positivity long enough, and you create a positive reality. One that challenges how they think sharpens their mind. A loving heart brings joy to its environment. Emotions can be contagious. If someone looks up to you, you could help mentally shape them. Sometimes the weighing of priorities at the right time is the solution. Three X factors in creating peace are: a good heart, mental stability, and strong will power. One could choose to be happy in any metaphorical boat they are in.

A searching heart wonders much. A curious mind finds answers, just make sure you're curious about the right things, because not all answers are soothing to the soul. A divine message carries more volume than cunning words.

Truth can heal hearts or break them. Love can keep a person sane; the loss of love can drive them crazy. Many fear a wicked king, but a righteous one is loved by the majority of his kingdom. It can be detrimental to compare lives. Could one rightfully judge if their life is ultimately fair or unfair? For one aspect that someone is cursed in, another they could be blessed in. For instance, in my opinion, I never should have found myself in this metaphorical boat I'm in now, but if I didn't then I probably never would have written this book. Sometimes what we interpret as a tribulation can be a blessing in disguise. Rejection can be a good thing: for instance, you ask out someone that you think is perfect for you, but they reject you. Later, you might find someone who is actually perfect for you, not knowing that the one that previously rejected you would have been wrong for you.

A loving home can mend a broken heart. In the bible it says, "Pride before the fall," one shouldn't let their ego get the best of them, because the result will be them metaphorically hitting rock bottom. Always be humble and kind.

One speech could end a war, although the speech would have to be very divine, profound, and powerful. The one that would be successful in creating peace will see things from all angles. Metaphorical friction is created when no middle ground exists. The lack of vision can result in wasted talent. A vivid vision might be the root of a revolution, but it is fueled through strong motivation. Your memories and your accomplishments will be your footprint on the earth. Too much love for change can be the cause of an unfaithful person, sometimes one should learn to appreciate what they have. Some go their whole lives trying to create one powerful memory. If you have one true friend in life, you're lucky: true friendship is priceless. Everyone wants to feel a sense of security; some that's been deprived of it might go to dramatic measures to obtain it. Our actions, words, and intent can change how God works in our lives. Every choice has an outcome. The one that understands both sides of an argument, but is at a loss for words, feels spiritually torn. When one betters their perception, they increase their likelihood of gaining goodness. The Holy Spirit is nurturing to the soul. The one that aims to fulfill their purpose is Christ driven, the one that fulfills it receives an abundance of joy.

Recognizing God's works fortifies faith. Sometimes one has to become broken in order to be fixed. With guidance a wild youth can transition to wisdom with age. A wise person can make a complex message sound simple and give a simple message more volume. Insightful is the one who knows how to reach out to a variety of different people. Show another enough love and you can convert their heart. Achieving a task can feel rewarding, while failing one feels disappointing. Be original, remember there's only one of you. The minds that seek in depth answers loves to ponder. Solve a mystery and you can change the world. The power of the Holy Spirit triumphs all other powers. There is no real freedom without freewill. Everyone seeks to have a spiritual fire (powerful zeal) once you get it, don't let the devil put it out. Everyone dies, but not everyone lives. A righteous plan is the root of a positive movement. A humble prayer carries weight. A good heart, in alignment with a good perception, and hope, betters others. One who helps a righteous person receives favor from God. Spiritually good fruit nurtures the soul. Would you rather hear a gentle lie, or a hard truth? Because a true friend will tell you the truth no matter what, due to the fact that he or she loves you. Doubt mentally cripples.

You never know what someone else can become. It takes power to have an immense effect, but there's a big difference in wanting to have a huge effect and becoming obsessed with power: stay meek and humble. Hearing the right message can change a life. We all go through a metaphorical dry spell (when our thoughts don't click, we don't feel God's love and presence: it feels like there's a barrier, and it seems impossible to grow,) maybe God is seeing how we respond? I believe He still wants us to turn toward Him, and keep doing what is right, but He has to know if we will still do that even when it becomes a hard thing to do.

God will provide more to those that do great with what they have. Joy is found when positive thinking is used, and the time is right. Don't pass down hate, be a good influence. Everyone wants peace at one point in time, but the loss of hope can rob one from the desire to want peace: the abundance of hope is in alignment with the abundance of love. One should find a good balance between work and play: too much of either is bad.

Seek to achieve the right things, for accomplishment of the wrong things can feel like imprisonment of the soul. Don't let your tragedies define you, one should always strive to be a better person. The one with stronger will, can outdo the one with more talent. When someone says you are what you eat, they mean: you are what you mentally digest, what we choose to focus on shapes our soul. A wiseman aims to put himself in the best environment as possible. A wiseman obtains good company.

Chapter Four

Different Definitions

Different people could have different definitions of what's normal to them: for instance, some might think peace is normal, while others could think violence is normal. It isn't always easy to love someone. When a parent loves their child, sometimes they have to correct them, as a result their kid might get mad at them, but should know that their parent is only doing it because they love them. A divine message can blossom a listener's soul.

The combination of being open minded, insightful, and knowledgeable creates wisdom. Learning a useful skill might bring more opportunities: but try to do what you love, because loving your job is priceless. I say kindness is power, for instance: who is stronger, a person with a hundred friends, or one with a hundred enemies? Balancing optimism and realism is a logical take on life, but with the right amount of faith, the impossible is defied.

A bitter soul that's lost hope in their own dream will be more likely to discourage another's. Peace of mind is true freedom; serenity comes from God. Happy is the person that finds his purpose, if achieved; blessed is the memory of them. Everyone envies the hope of a kid. Good creativity is better than learned facts.

God wants to spiritually set you free, let the Holy Spirit into your heart and your desires will change you'll feel better than you ever imagined. One that desires to spread joy is of good fruit. It is better to have love in your heart but have little; then to have an abundance but only know hate. Doing good deeds in this life builds treasure in heaven, and refraining from evil pleases God. Plentiful are the good thoughts of an upright person. God's messengers must keep a stable mind, because when they thirst, others will try to get them to drink from the cup of controversy, just to destroy their purpose. Every

Saint was once a sinner. The Holy Spirit will reveal the true nature of other people's souls. It refers to Jesus as being the light of the world, because like light he directs your path, yeah life still might put obstacles in your way, but as long as you got his light in your life, you can see them and you won't stumble. Corruption reaps suffering, love reaps joy. Good will reaps hope, wickedness reaps pain and remorse. Pointing out other people's faults doesn't shield yours.

If someone doesn't know you, they will judge you based off who you hang out with: if you know you're good and wise enough to make your environment a product of you, be prepared to temporarily sacrifice your reputation, but if successful you'll receive honor. Happy is a person who falls in love, remorseful is a person who loses it. Don't let your affliction blind you, keep an open mind. In the presence of an upright person, one is at ease: in the presence of an evil person, one stays on their toes. Sometimes the smallest input has the greatest output, (or effect-outcome.) One must fall short numerous times before becoming victorious. The path of a champion is a rough road. Before one's spiritual cup can be filled, they must follow Christ.

Don't let sin destroy you, or separate you from God, if one falls short, be quick to repent. One must find it in them to forgive themselves. According to 1 Corinthians 13:13 "for there is faith, hope, and love, but the greatest of these is love." Now it mentions these three things because they work in unison; for one, you need the other two. Be the change in the world you want to see. An empire wasn't built in a day. God constantly provides us with opportunities: the harder the situation, the harder it is to see the opportunity. Time is more precious than wealth. A degree of life is made up of fate, but most of it is defined by one's own will. The heart's intentions transition into how the mind functions. Your true self will be revealed overtime. God is the ultimate judge. One that seeks to fulfill their purpose and be understood over fame and fortune, is of a humble and kind nature. Blessed is he who assembles good company. Fruitful are the acts of salvation. An old righteous man receives an abundance of joy. Good are the encounters of the faithful. Heavy is the load of the wicked. The man that gets his priories straight becomes more prosperous than the man that has them disarranged. The hardening of the heart cripples one's ability to understand.

Ones life is made up of a lot of different stages, for in one stage you might desire to do one thing, while in another you could possess a totally different desire; desires can change over time. Timing is important, you can relay the same message to someone at two different points in time and get two different results. One can only disguise the nature of one's soul for so long: in length of words the heart is revealed. One chooses what they believe and what they disregard. One of my favorite quotes' states: "with great power comes great responsibility." See your tribulations as God's refinement and be proud. Good is the person who puts other people's needs above their own, wise is the one who knows when the appropriate time to do so exists. Wise is the person who knows to lead by example, upright is the one who does. Good intent matters, but isn't the whole product of a righteous person, for perspective plays a role. For it is written, "a house that's divided can't stand:" the devil will try to even use your good qualities against you. A person should be careful as to what they look and pray for: for one can find the very things they seek. Everyone's knowledge put together, couldn't even compete with God's wisdom. It is better to be low in this life, but to later be accepted into God's kingdom: then to be rich in this life but never see the streets of gold. People fear the unknown, but God spiritually moves through us best when we venture out unto that realm: God defies the impossible. Faith establishes one's limits. Persistency is a characteristic of a champion.

God will present more opportunities to the ones that overcome their hardships. A blessing are those of the offspring of the upright. Pleasing are the prayers of the righteous. Abundant thoughts are the product of a faithful heart. For one's belief is the structure of one's reality. When a person looks for unity, they seek their purpose. God is the provider and taker of intellect: put your faith in the supplier of knowledge, and not within the knowledge itself. Freewill can be a gift and/or a curse, choose wisely. The devil is the master of confusion. Don't let bad past experiences influence pre-judgement of a stranger. Happy is the one that receives forgiveness. Through Christ there's redemption for all, but one must be willing to receive it. One should pray to become an instrument of God's will. God loves a gentle heart, but the acts of intimidation, He despises. Meekness is praised, and the power of love is limitless. Men's categories don't determine God's plan, for He chooses to use people from all walks of life. Men might label you, but God searches one's heart and see's one's soul, and not the image of your flesh. In the eyes of the wise, inner beauty triumphs over outward appearance.

For it is written, "You reap what you sow," in knowing this, one should be willing to please karma, but the goodness you put out must come from a genuine source, (do things for the right reason, not just to expect a reward.) Normally good deeds produce joy. A true friend sticks by your side, even at your lowest point in life. Jesus' disciples might have been his followers, but they were also leaders.

Every leader at one point in time is rejected. Everyone wants to be a legend, but no one wants to go through what it takes to become one.

To measure an idea, evaluate the fruit of its product. Happiness is a state of mind. Believe in yourself and you'll be more likely to achieve your goals. Truth can heal or destroy. Wisdom can change lives. The love of knowledge is good, but don't make gaining wisdom your only priority. Faith can make prosperity more attainable. Love changes people. If you look at the glass as being half full then you'll be more likely to fill it up. A hungry mind has more potential than someone who thinks they know it all. Great is the weight of a king. Challenge your mind and you can beat the odds. Don't let someone else determine your worth, establish yourself. Power can feel like a curse or a blessing.

Sometimes God uses who we view as the most unusual people: my example, the apostle Paul from the bible. Good principles create obedient people, which establishes loyalty, which makes the world better. Opportunities come in time, so seize the moment. Knowledge is like a flower, if you water it then with time it grows. Most people wish their life away, then toward the end try to wish it back: but you'll never get today back, so enjoy it while you can. Seize the moment. Free spirited people are more likely to become happy. Staying worried is depressing. Truly examine yourself, realize what you want to achieve, get your priorities in order. Those who chase their dreams and unravel a mystery, find happiness as an outcome. What one considers to be a mystery; another could consider to be part of their common sense. Everyone is unique in certain ways but have similar basic desires. A humble soul, constructive mind, and generous heart create a kind being that's capable of changing the world. A bad teacher and bad student create chaos. A good teacher and bad student create misunderstanding. But a good teacher and good student create a fruitful person. Learn to laugh at life, or life will learn to laugh at you. Your life can be changed in a moment. If you non-violently work out your issues, then you better your circumstance.

Patience can be key, but not always is, one should know when to utilize patience and wait for something, and when to seize the moment. Joy can save a lost soul. Money can change people. Power and influence go hand and hand. The root of a revolution is strong will. "Strong men create good times, good times create weak men, weak men create hard times, and hard times create strong men."

Chapter Five

Respect

Respect yourself in moderation and others will be more likely to respect you. It's good to give others a base line of respect and see if you can trust them with it. Respect is valuable. speech is admired. Elegant words and ideas transform minds. I see disabilities as obstacles to overcome. Prayer is spiritual warfare artillery. Understand someone's values, principles, and desires, and you understand them.

Finding love can be amazing but losing it can be terrible. The devil comes against the strongest when you're the weakest: keep faith, stay in prayer. When you're feeling discouraged, it is the most important time to pray. In the end God honors righteousness. Life is a process; one should grow in faith and understanding. Learn from the hard times, embrace the good, and establish yourself in the neutral. The higher you fly, the further you'll fall. Life can feel like a rollercoaster, it has its ups, and downs, and everything in-between. It is woeful to brag and boast. One that keeps their composure when enraged demonstrates mental strength and stability. Happiness is a product of genuine love. Heaven is the reward of a righteous person. Acceptance is a main infrastructure of equality. Unity is the social goal. When a man's expectations are met or surpassed, happy is he. It is easier to teach a kid righteousness, then it is to convert a man. Grace is the product of sincere repentance. Prayer is the infrastructure of faith. There are different forms of wisdom; acknowledge what form of intellect it is you seek, and I pray the path to find it is the one you take. Powerful are the words of the wise, one should listen to them intently. As long as you're successful in carrying your metaphorical load; the heavier it is, the stronger you'll spiritually become. God won't give you more than what you can handle, but while in the valley it seems as if He did.

God's power has no limits. Good judgement of a person comes through the nature of their plan. For it is written, "in the end God will pour out knowledge upon his people," I believe this is a generation were epiphanies come in abundance. Powerful prayer, in alignment with strong faith, results in dramatic change and/or miracles. Jesus is the rock of salvation, if you seek a sharp mind, then place your thoughts upon the rock. A vengeful heart covers a multitude of love: but the abundance of love can fix a vengeful heart. The chosen ones have a dramatic effect. The best victory comes from the avoided war.

Speed is a stronger attribute than strength. It is better to make peace, than provoke war. One that finds solutions is stronger than one that makes trouble. One that has a good perspective receives honor. Powerful are the meek, withheld is their force, focus is their strength. Mental stability is sharpened when one keeps their composure during a hardship. It says to pray for thine enemy for multiple reasons, two most important are, you don't know what they are going through and why they act that way could be the devil working through them: and if God changes their heart, who knows, they could morph into becoming the most loving person you know.

If a man is content at the low points of his life, how much more zealous do you think he'll be at his peaks? If a man is loving when going through lives valleys, could words describe how he'll be during life's high points? Great is the load of a righteous king, ignorant is the mind of a wicked one. Even kings shall bow to Christ. Woe to an evil king, for his very servant could be his judge. God is everywhere, for God is the omnipresent spirit. Men call it your conscience, and it is that peaceful, still voice one hears when they're little; it tells them right from wrong, convicts one when they've done wrong. My question is, what do you think the source of that voice is? Could it be God's voice? Mankind has been around for a real long time, now in our galaxy we have an asteroid belt, comets, meteors etc. with all these things floating around, what's the likelihood that something hasn't hit this planet and wiped us out yet? Slim to none, right? I believe it's more logical to believe that God exist and oversees everything, then it is to disprove His existence.

For I've witnessed miracles, I am a miracle, and God is working through me to bring you all this Knowledge: He wants to work through us all, Amen. Great is one who acknowledges God's inner workings. Wise is the one that places insight over riches. One reason why people say that someone that has intense passion has a fire inside is because fire spreads.

A person's memory is more powerful than the wealth they leave behind. Seize the moment. Don't wish the current moment away, for you don't know what the next one is to bring. The past is history, the futures a mystery, and the present's a gift. The presence of the righteous is a blessing. The nature of the cause normally results in the fruit of the product, but if your heart tells you otherwise, then listen to it. Although good intentions can and should produce good results, that's not always the case, a clear perspective plays a role, along with other things. The bond of the righteous is impenetrable, the bond of the wicked can be broken through fear. Most words that proceed out of the mouth of the righteous are that of life, most of the wicked words are that of death: but everyone's good to a degree, one should try to bring the best out of others and present the best version of themselves. A person's upbringing contributes greatly to who they become, but remember, everyone who ever lived had freewill. What God ordains, the devil can't destroy, unless that person spiritually opens the door to Satan: God's plan will over-ride.

If everyone else in the world was crazy to different degrees, then wouldn't they view the only sane one as being insane? Everyone seems to want to give advice but never take none. Better is he who is strong but stays humble and meek: then he that is weak but has a short temper. 'You can lead a horse to water, but you can't make him drink.' Patience is a virtue. A powerful heart can fix a dysfunctional mind, depending on the degree of the heart's power, will determine the degree of the mental miracle.

Sometimes one might want to take more fault on a cause if the actual scenario behind the cause makes one sound out of their mind. A lazy man wishes away his time, but productive time is soothing to the soul. An appetite for spiritual fulfillment, will produce an overflowing cup: allow your trials to build the armor of God. A clear mind is the product of focusing on the right things and putting your faith in God. Casting out the spirit of doubt when it comes against, results in stronger faith. Be content with who you are, for you don't know if you could fit another's shoes; focus on the role God has given you. No one should ever want to end their life on this page, for you don't know what the next chapter of your life will hold. Woe to those that cause trouble; but great are the peace makers. Good deeds, when done with good intent, make God happy. One that whispers lies, has a corrupt heart. Loyalty is ultimately good, but it is bad to be loyal to the wrong cause.

When God sends a message through a person, the words flow like a river. Focus your heart on the right things, for the love of the bad things is a sin within itself: for instance, the love of money is detrimental to the soul. Christ teaches us how to have life, and life more abundantly: one has to sacrifice bad habits and wrong thinking in order for them to create an abundant life for themselves. Great are the acts of the faithful. A good spirit forms discernment.

A priceless moment can be worth a week of despair, depending on the element of despair. Our reality is found somewhere in between our destiny, and our own freewill. One that stays productive during a hardship is an innovator: one that transforms a tribulation into a blessing is a child of God. One that stays positive, is of good spirit, seeks a change for the better, and/or creates blessings. If one can acknowledge God's goodness, even in the valleys of life: He'll be generous enough to make their future prosperous. God can transform the worse of the worse, into the best of the best: my example will be, the apostle Paul. Beyond ocean depths, are the thoughts of the chosen ones: but credit goes to God. Open your mind to God, and He will transform your reality. Prosperity is the result of strong will and strong faith. Hope creates determination. Love triumphs over hate. Good perspective forms love. One shouldn't be jealous, because it transitions into hate, and having hate in your heart is a sin within itself. Pure are the desires of a child, one that up brings them right gets rewarded by them later on in life.

Gentle are the acts of the meek: humble, but powerful are God's Shepard's. Wolves might be quick, but God's Shepard's are like lightning. One of God's messengers wings are formed through their obedience to Him. Their words are their feathers. Great is the structure of the righteous. Abundance are the offspring of the fruitful. The wise feel merry for the principles they've been taught. Insight is to be passed down, wisdom is to be shared with the ones you love. People will let you down, but God's love never fails. Your perspective, in response to a situation, determines the emotion felt. When God speaks through a person, others are morphed, acts of God create miracles, and in comparison, the works of the flesh are minute. When the road is ventured down far enough: amazed are those that followed God. God, I gave you an empty cup, yes you made me wait, but when you returned it, it was overflowing. Amazed are those that acknowledge God's wisdom. Blessed is the one that obeys God, Pure are those that hear His calm and peaceful voice. God can manifest Himself into any image He desires, the image one sees when they see Him, will be the image that they accept most. In the scriptures it states that He came down in the spirit of a dove when Jesus was being baptized by John. He came down in that form because a dove signifies purity and love. Misunderstanding God creates violence, while understanding Him creates peace. One that helps another is upright: one that knows who to help is both upright and wise. One should remember not to cast their pearls among swine. Good are the intentions of a babe, evil are the ones that corrupt them. This world is the devil's playground. Tough experiences can be blessings in disguise. Maturity is in alignment with wisdom. Insight expands one's horizons. One who thinks outside the box, sees things from all angles.

Chapter Six

Feed the Right Wolf

You can't have sunshine all the time, because then you get a drought. Having downs in life helps you appreciate the good in life. Look at the struggles in life as a humbling experience. Balance is key, too much of a good thing is a bad thing. Rain literally creates growth. Perspective changes everything. Friction creates fire, fire creates transformation. The heat and pressure of your trials can turn a coal into a diamond. Peace is formed when a middle ground is established. Don't get in such a hurry to get to where you're going, that you overlook where you're at now: for your present situation could be better than your future.

To understand one's actions sometimes you must see through their eyes. Hope is found where love exists. Don't let anyone tell you that you can't achieve a goal before you even try; first attempt it, then later evaluate your progress. The key to your own success lies within yourself, but you have got to believe first and foremost. One appreciates the things they had to work to receive more than the things that were just given to them. Being friendly to difficult people shows character. Good spiritual vision and good intent create righteousness.

Freedom comes at a price: freedom isn't free. A long weary road is that of a champion. A well-executed righteous plan is beneficial to those involved: for example, if you open up a food pantry in your town and end up feeding a lot of people in need, that's obviously helpful to those people. A scholar of God is a leader of men. Everyone has a weakness or Achilles heel, thoroughly knowing yourself is how you work through your own personal issues: but personal insight in this form is key to finding out how to solve your own issues. Listen to your instincts, very rarely do they mislead you: follow your heart, it's a good guide. When you feel unsure about something, pray and seek God's guidance. "To act globally, you got to think locally."

A grateful person receives more blessings than someone who takes everything for granted. One should pray for God to give them more wisdom and show them favor. It is better to have great faith and strong determination than good skills and pride. Stay optimistic, for your dreams could be easier to achieve than you initially thought. Take it from me: after my car accident my intellect was mostly taken away for a few years. I had to put immense faith in God for it to be restored, not only did He restore it, but He added to it nicely. Now I believe that the intellectual trail I faced after my car accident was a test of my faith. Who are we to question why God does certain things?

Blessed is the one who sees opportunity in almost everything. You can't be good at everything: for one thing I'm bad at, there's another thing I'm good at. God will provide us with the tools we need to get by or solve a problem; we just got to use the tools He supplies us with. If you don't like the harvest, plant different seeds: if you don't like the situation then change your perspective and words; speak victory, not defeat or the problem. Learn from your trials and you'll more than likely move on, but repeating mistakes leaves you stagnant. Those that are open-minded learn more than a close-minded person does. When one loses their meaning to life, their mind enters a civil war.

Good teamwork outdoes great individual performance. Learn from your past in order to better your future. When your mind is at war with itself, the choices you make are detrimental. Black pepper is surprisingly really good for you; it even helps your brain function. From the words of Linkin Park, "when the rich wage war, it's the poor that die." Finding a healthy balance of activities is essential, for one can get bored from doing the same thing over and over again. If everyone goes the extra yard, it saves someone a mile. Food for thought heals the soul.

Once I heard an old Indian wise tale, and it stated: there were a grandfather Chief talking to his grandson, and he told him that everyone has two wolves inside of them, and these wolves are at constant battle: one is of light, (the good wolf) and one is of darkness, (the bad wolf) the grandson asked his grandfather, which one wins the battle? The grandfather replied, "The one you feed the most".

Learn to love your enemies and you'll surely love your friends. You can't sweep everything under the rug, after a while your afflictions will haunt you. One programs their mind how to think: create a positive algorithm and you'll get a chain of positive thoughts, or vice versa. Productive time equals satisfaction, while wasted time equals regret. A thirst for knowledge is temporally quenched when epiphanies occur. Achievement of milestones is nurturing to the soul. Everybody's a stranger at one point in time. If someone keeps wronging you, maybe it's best to avoid them.

Perspective varies, everyone sees things differently. If you think outside the box, you could acknowledge how a situation could be seen in a different light, or different way. Everyone should have a desire to do better. Doing good things with the right intentions is a good start. But be cautious because the devil will try to even use your good intent against you: for example, the apostle Paul; before he became known as Paul, he was known as Saul, and he was persecuting Christians. He thought he was doing God's will because he thought Jesus and His followers where blaspheming God, but that wasn't the case.

Sobriety is worth the struggle of fighting the urge to use; you put yourself in better situations and you keep a clear mindset.

Don't let anyone deprive you of hope, hope is essential. Remember, everyone changes the world to a degree. You affect the people you're around, and the ones that love you: your effect on them could alter their effect on others. (Even the biggest fires are started by a spark.) Your purpose could even be way more immense than you think: 'The Creator doesn't call the equipped, He equips the called." The ones that have the biggest roles to play in life, end up facing the biggest struggles, and sadly but true others try to discourage them the most.

When we place a stigma on someone, we basically set them up for failure. When you feed someone with negative ideology, they're more prone to fail. With the right amount of hope and good mind set limits break, but stigmas rob people of hope and create unhealthy mind sets.

Chapter Seven

A True Conversion

God can convert anyone, but some people are so lost that they don't allow Him to convert them. One's belief determines how God works in their life. Limitless power is the product of strong faith. Epiphanies are the product of a walking miracle. Pleasing is the legacy of a meek person, terrible is the one of the wicked. One should thrive to present the best version of themselves. When tested by the devil, turn toward God. The chosen ones have the most influence, but everyone has freewill: that's why the devil comes against them the hardest. The power of insight, wisdom, and understanding is massive, for the right combination of the three creates immense persuasion. With enough persuasion, one can rule an empire. But this element of persuasion comes from a higher power. The Almighty God triumphs over evil. Like how the light eliminates the dark. Everyone faces their Creator one day. In that day one will feel a mixture of emotions. One will stand in front of the Throne of Judgement, just like how a hearing takes place in court: Jesus will be their lawyer, the saints will be their jury, Satan will be their Prosecuting Attorney, and God the Almighty will be their judge, and He has the final say so.

True love is when one loves another based off of who they are, and not what they have to give. Rich are the righteous, for they got a spot in God's Kingdom. What good is a profound message if you don't understand the meaning? Sometimes one should find the balance between being simple and complex. True love is radiant. If you want it to last, then put Christ first. A lot of the time God works through people, allow Him to work through you and joy will come in abundance.

Everyone comes to a metaphorical fork in the road, there's two main paths to life, and everyone knows where each path ultimately leads to: why wouldn't one take the path that leads to heaven? Turn toward God and the spirit of confusion will be broken, the chains of sinful desire will seize to exist, and your   prison will vanish. The devil gives one the spirit of fear, while God's spirit makes one brave, bold; but humble and kind: as graceful as the steps of a lion, as generous as a charity, as strong as Samson, and as wise as Solomon. Great is the one that focuses on righteous things.

There's a fine line between bravery and stupidity. Determination is the structure of a champion. Hang around people that challenge how you think. Everyone is unique to a degree. Successful becomes the one that knows what advice to disregard, and what advice to take and when to take it. Wise is the one who sees a situation from every angle: insightful is the one who can explain how the situation can be seen from a different angle. Most view insight over knowledge and understanding over flattering words. Capture someone's interest, and you'll win their heart. Reason with another to find common ground.

Most religions are fruit from the same tree: Jesus is the messiah. Good moral conduct is essential. One should remember the law of the prophets: 'Love the Lord thy God with all thine heart and love thy neighbor as thine self" That is the backbone of religion. Being the best version of yourself is the goal of spirituality: the backbone of it is embracing God's love. We all play a part to a bigger picture. A clear mind is the product of a loving heart. A taste of God's brilliance intrigues everybody.

The stars in the sky are like the grains of sand on the beach; although there's so much out there, God's awesome enough to hear your every prayer; He cares about you more than you'll ever know. Sometimes one is to wait for change, but most of the time they are to make the change: wise is the person who acknowledges when they should wait, and when they should take action. Powerful are the thoughts of the wise. Your purpose is in alignment with your desire. Those that stay prepared don't have to get ready. One's actions should fall in accord with their belief The one that leads by example has more of an influence than one that presents flattering words: but great is the one who walks and talks positively. One should refrain from lies only say what you mean. People will respect you more if you just simply be yourself. There are elements of good in everyone, God wants you to flourish, while the devil wants to destroy you: let me encourage you to come into the light.

You can't teach hustle. A marathon starts by a step. If you're passionate about what you do, then you'll be more likely to improve. Jealousy fogs the mind. Everyone desires to win, the way you win matters. Powerful is the hope of a kid, one should transition their hope into strong faith. One day, after we die, and right before we get to the Throne of Judgement; we will walk with our savior to the Throne; oh, what an amazing conversation we'll have, what an amazing feeling it'll be to walk beside you Jesus, my Lord. This is the time to turn toward God, for the hour is near: may your perspective be true, your intent be pure, your words be that of life, your heart be filled with love, and your spirit be strong in faith.

The road to greatness is a weary road, don't let others discourage you while following its path. Strong independence is power, but strong faith in God Almighty is more immense. One should be rooted in faith, but to ensure that their roots isn't plucked up when the storm hits, they should be thriving to grow in spirituality, and in God's goodness. The scriptures of the righteous penetrate the heart of their foes. The words of the upright, open a listener's heart, but the devil tries to steal acknowledgement from he that hears God's word. The power of change lies within oneself, allow God to work through thee. Face your trials with a triumphant heart. Waiting for division is like waiting for a snare placed upon the soul. Waiting for the seasons is like waiting for the leaves to fall back upon the trees. Great is the faith of a kid, altered is the faith of a dual minded man. Happy is the path of the faithful, upright is the path of the weary: for strong is the product of their endurance. Plentiful are a seed of believers. Powerful are the upright, for their ways are pleasing; and their path is straight and narrow. Love was bought through Calvary but is obtained through righteousness.

In time a pure hearted prayer gets answered, as long as the prayers are for your benefit. The path of the wicked is rough, the path of the holy is prosperous. The challenges of the chosen are immense, for their purpose is divine. The ocean of doubt has an under tide called fear: turn toward God and he won't just keep you afloat, he'll get you out of that body of water and put you on the rock of salvation.

Happy are the ways of the righteous, for their path is a product of their faith. Proceed with caution for the hour is at hand. Great is the infrastructure of a humble plan. Wisdom is the product of strong faith and good perspective. Insight's a product of elastic thought. Understanding is a product of good listening and reasoning. God is the supplier of all things. We are all God's children, but some have chosen to turn against him.

One should value success over riches alone: for one can accumulate more money than they will ever know how to spend. If/when one realizes that others are just considering them a friend because of the things they have, and the materials they provide: a sad reality is what they face. Lonely are the ones that don't have God in their heart, and don't know of the love of Christ. There will be times when people let you down, other times when things go wrong and possessions mess up: even guns jam at times; but God is faithful toward the righteous. In the grand scheme of things, His people will be victorious. God, my faith has been tested and it's endured and grown tremendously: others have tried to steal my hope, at once it felt withered, but you fortified it: through my hard times you gave me a testimony; and at one point in time, you took my intellect, but now has made me brilliant beyond measure. My God, The Almighty, The Father of Christ, the God of Abraham, Isaac, and Jacob, the Creator of the heavens and the earths, the omnipresent spirit, my redeemer, the Alpha and Omega; you know my heart, my hope is upon you, may everyone who reads this be blessed beyond measure. May they accept these words of yours and acknowledge the truth. May I be successful in pointing them toward Jesus: who is my Lord, savior, the messiah, and my best friend. Thanks for providing me with these thoughts and may these beautiful words you've passed on open every spiritual eye in the world. For you know my intent is for everyone to feel the joy you've supplied me with, for I feel like a tree planted beside fresh water. Amen

Chapter Eight

Mental Fitness

The human mind is an incredible instrument. Will power can knock down mental barriers. Full-heartedly devoting yourself to a task can have a dramatic effect: you could achieve more than what you or anyone else ever dreamed possible. Tim Duncan has a quote that fits this logic pretty well, and that is, "hard work beats talent when talent don't work hard".

Personally, I've dealt with quite a bit of negative outlooks and unexpected criticism from my mom and classmates, (back when I was in school.) This temporarily hindered my determination to bounce back from my traumatic brain injury that I suffered from a car accident back in 2004. But eventually I worked up the motivation to put forth the effort to start challenging my mind by applying myself to whatever I did, I call this mental fitness.

Although my cognitive ability started improving due to this mental fitness, I seen a dramatic increase once I started writing lyrics and stories, playing sports, and instruments: I still find this helpful because it is a great stimulation for the mind.

There are so many depths of wisdom, I see it as there's different plateaus. Now it's inevitable, we all are on different levels of wisdom, but just like how one can climb a ladder, one can use mental fitness to progress intellectually.

Don't let societies labels control your own personal insight on how you view yourself, for instance, they even thought Albert Einstein was stupid because he had dyslexia and they didn't know anything about that disorder back then. But Einstein turned out to be a genius.

You never know what you can do until you start doing it. Take the first step.

Chapter Nine

Different Countries Point of View

Every country's history class is modified to make their own county look the best it can. No country is perfect; every nation has done some good and some bad. 'When the rich wage war, it's the poor that die.' Good people are spread out through the world. Even if you hate a specific country, you probably hate that county based off how the people that control it run it, if you go to war with that county, you're fighting a totally different group of people than the ones that run it. Those people you're fighting are fighting too: either because they need a job, or because their country has presented the reason for the war from a totally different angle and has won their loyalty, or both. We might be from different parts of the world, but we could be more similar than you think. No one controls where they're from.

Chapter Ten

My Views on Racism

Judging a group of people based on the color of their skin makes no sense. Better yet, the Bible tells us to 'pray for thine enemy,' because we don't know what anyone goes through, or went through. I have met good and bad people of every race. I believe we're all the same inside. We probably were all fed bad stigmas that tell us other races are "this" or "that," but not only are those stigmas wrong, they have severely affected our world in a negative way. Choose LOVE instead of hate.

Chapter Eleven

My Testimony

A couple weeks before my 11th birthday my grandma asked me if I wanted to go to a church camp, but my response surprised her, for it was no. Now understand that at that point in time I didn't even know if God existed, and I figured if He did, He was cruel/cold hearted: for I was an excellent child but had an abundance of hardships, while I witnessed some others that were bad and/or didn't believe, but had it good. Plus, my Grandma was my epitome of a Christian, and she would force her religion upon me, and back then I thought she was crazy. I figured if religion did that to her, then I want no part of it. Nevertheless, she made me go to church camp.

Honestly, I don't remember much of the speech my Grandma gave to my sister as we headed to that church camp, for it has been a long time ago that this happened, but I do remember that she told her that, "sex before marriage was a sin." Later I found out that God let me hear that to test my morality down the road.

The church camp was in Doniphan, Missouri. When we got there our Grandma informed us that we had a cousin named Trevor that'll be attending the camp as well, and she ended up introducing us. Here we were talking and getting to know each other, while also observing all the other people that were there, and the ones coming in. There were these two girls that kept coming back toward the entrance area, I didn't notice the attention given, until my cousin mentioned it: "hey Nathan, that girl over there keeps staring at you, I think she might find you attractive."

I look to where he points and respond, "oh, the cute one?"

He answers, "Yes."

"I say we go talk to them." So, we went and talked to the two girls and not long after I had my first kiss, and so on and so forth.

During the first sermon the pastor claimed to have had a vision 5 nights in a row about someone getting in an accident and having a death/to near death experience. He went on to reveal his intent, and that was to spiritually save their soul before the accident.

Now honestly, I was thinking that this sounded like a whole lot of BS, in other words, I thought he was lying. But I pondered, and as I thought it occurred to me that it was possible that he was telling the truth; for at that time God would give me a lot of visions. Honestly, most of them seemed like they were of no importance, but now I believe that He gave them to me, so I would question his existence at that moment.

So now I realized, it was possible that he had this vision, but what was the likelihood that it was of me? Very slim, for there must have been 250 kids in that congregation. So, I had conflicting thoughts, I was confused, and my doubt seemed like it was on a rollercoaster: so, I started observing how everyone else was responding, and they were fearful. They were hitting their knees and praying. Finally, I thought, why don't I feel like that, as my thoughts went wild. So, I prayed, "God if you exist then prove yourself, for you know my heart, and know that I got to know if you really exist."

A few days past, and since God didn't send me a sign or answer yet: I swore He didn't exist. So, I was sitting down while everyone else was standing and rejoicing, for I was disappointed and mad.

Finally, my cousin Trevor turned toward me and told me to stand, that I looked so out of place, others thought I was retarded. I told him that to me they were the ones that looked retarded, for they were reaching out for God, when He didn't exist. Then my cousin responded, "Maybe you're right, maybe you're wrong. But I can feel something great moving right now, you should give it a try and see if you feel it too."

I thought for a moment and responded, "Why don't I feel it?"

My cousin looked shocked, "You don't feel it because you're not putting forth any effort, and you got to meet God halfway. You never know until you try." (That response changed my life.)

I stood up and started trying to feel the joy everyone else felt, but honestly, I didn't feel it then: so I was about to sit back down when I saw what I thought was the sign I prayed for. There were two kids walking back from the altar. One was crying, and the other had a huge smile on his face. Now I remember seeing these two kids when they arrived here at this camp; and they looked so depressed then, but now not only did they look happy, but I never saw anyone look so joyful.

It hit me hard; I received an epiphany. I swore this was the answer to my prayer. I was so eager to feel what they felt and determined to create an everlasting relationship with God now that I knew He existed. I sprinted to the front, weaved through the other kids that where high on the Holy Spirit, I grabbed the pastor, banged on my chest, and shouted, "Pray for me!"

The pastor was in shock as he said, "Oh my God, you're that kid." But he turned back and continued to pray for this other girl.

I pushed him, and said firmly, "You must have not heard me old man, I told you to pray for me." He laid his hand on my head and began to pray for me. Immediately I felt the presence of the Holy Spirit, for I felt better than I ever did before.

Circling back to that girl I mentioned I met at the beginning of the church camp: we became a thing, we would sneak off and make out every chance we got; Then after the last service she came up and told me to meet her outside the girl's bathroom at 10:00 p.m. but I had no idea what she had in mind.

Nevertheless, we met up that night. But when I tried to kiss her, she pushed me back and told me that we should have sex. I won't lie, I wanted to: but I remember what my Grandma had said before dropping me and my sister off, and I remember how I had the realization that God was real. And at that point in time, I felt like if I had sex with her then that it would be like metaphorically spitting in God's face. So, I lowered my head and told her that I wanted to, but it wouldn't feel like the right thing to do, then I explained why.

She looked like she was a little let down, but she understood and respected me. She told me that we should meet in the same spot tomorrow. She wanted me to meet her mom and exchange numbers.

But the next day came and I slept in, my cousin was trying to get me to hurry because my Grandma was waiting for me in the parking lot and was in a hurry to leave.

After I got ready, I tried to meet up with that girl, but my Grandma didn't allow it. See the girl's bathrooms were kind of on the way between my dorm and where my Grandma was, but it was off to the left. I started walking that way and my Grandma started yelling at me. I told her that I had to do something, but she thought I just had to go to the bathroom and told me that I could do that at the house. Although I said, "no I must do something" and kept yelling it across the distance that stood between us, she was persistent about leaving then: so I gave up and walked to the car.

The girl was yelling my name. My sister heard her, and as I came and got in the car, she asked me, "why the girl was calling for me".

I told her and my Grandma how, "I planned on getting her number and meeting her mom, that we were dating, and this was why I was headed that way and said I had something to do. But our Grandma was in too much of a hurry to care about me."

My Grandma got mad and drove off.

We went to her house so she could wash our clothes, then our stepmom took us to Walmart in Poplar Bluff, Missouri. It was June 19th, 2004, as we were headed home and going past the last gas station in Poplar Bluff headed north on Highway 67, a SUV was doing a burn out in the parking lot. My stepmom stopped in front of it, and it replaced where my door was.

I was on the back passenger side eating my candy when it happened. I remember looking at it approaching and feeling a state of complete helplessness. I was Air Evaced to St. Louis Children's Hospital, and I flat lined twice in the helicopter.

The doctors presented my mom with data that showed how unlikely it was that I'll make it and said: I would probably never regain consciousness again, and if I did, I would never walk and talk again. By the small chance that I beat those odds, it was basically inevitable: I would be extremely mentally impaired for the rest of my life. The doctors advised my mom that it'll be best just to pull the plug on my life support. But she didn't, instead she told the doctors that my God is bigger than this, He'll decide my son's fate and a lot of people prayed for me. She prayed that if God had a purpose for me, to bring me back but if not just to take me home.

I was in a coma for five days and awakened in the morning of June 24th, 2004, which happened to be my 11th birthday.

It had to be around midnight when I came to. My mom was asleep holding my hand. I opened my eyes for a split second, but it felt like lava was being poured on them. I tried to move, but I was too weak to do much. So, I lay there in my pain and anguish and prayed.

Finally, I squeezed my mom's hand a couple times, and she woke up, then I squeezed it again, and she started talking to me. I didn't have the strength yet to answer, but I squeezed her hand again.

I heard her call someone, and it must have been hours later when she started calling other people. It felt so long before the lights came on and sometime after I could hear people coming into the room.

Finally, I mustered up the strength to open my eyes, and I saw that the room was filled with my family and friends, and my birthday cake. We celebrated my birthday that day.

God proved the doctors wrong: for I did come back, I can walk and talk, and thanks to God I'm not mentally impaired. I asked for God to prove Himself, do you think He did?